Contents

Chipotle Chili

Makes 8 servings

Prep Time: 15 minutes   Cook Time: 8 hours

1 jar (16 ounces) Pace® Picante Sauce

1 cup water

2 tablespoons chili powder

1 teaspoon ground chipotle chile pepper

1 large onion, chopped (about 1 cup)

2 pounds beef for stew, cut into $\frac{1}{2}$-inch pieces

1 can (about 19 ounces) red kidney beans, rinsed and drained

   Shredded Cheddar cheese (optional)

   Sour cream (optional)

1. Stir the picante sauce, water, chili powder, chipotle pepper, onion, beef and beans in a $3\frac{1}{2}$-quart slow cooker.

2. Cover and cook on LOW for 8 to 9 hours* or until the beef is fork-tender. Serve with the cheese and sour cream, if desired.

Or on HIGH for 4 to 5 hours.

Golden Chicken with Noodles

Makes 8 servings

Prep Time: 5 minutes   *Cook Time: 7 hours*

2 cans (10³/₄ ounces *each*) Campbell's® Condensed Cream of Chicken Soup (Regular *or* 98% Fat Free)

¹/₂ cup water

¹/₄ cup lemon juice

1 tablespoon Dijon-style mustard

1¹/₂ teaspoons garlic powder

8 large carrots, thickly sliced (about 6 cups)

8 skinless, boneless chicken breast halves

¹/₂ of a 12-ounce package egg noodles (about 4 cups), cooked and drained

Chopped fresh parsley

1. Stir the soup, water, lemon juice, mustard, garlic powder and carrots in a 3¹/₂-quart slow cooker. Add the chicken and turn to coat.

2. Cover and cook on LOW for 7 to 8 hours* or until the chicken is cooked through. Serve with the noodles. Sprinkle with the parsley.

Or on HIGH for 4 to 5 hours.

Turkey Fajita Wraps

Makes 8 servings

Prep Time: 10 minutes   Cook Time: 6 hours

---

  2 cups Pace® Picante Sauce

  2 large green *or* red peppers, cut into 2-inch-long strips (about 4 cups)

1½ cups frozen whole kernel corn, thawed

  1 tablespoon chili powder

  2 tablespoons lime juice

  3 cloves garlic, minced

  2 pounds turkey breast cutlets, cut into 4-inch-long strips

16 flour tortillas (8-inch), warmed

     Shredded Mexican cheese blend

1. Stir the picante sauce, peppers, corn, chili powder, lime juice, garlic and turkey in a 4-quart slow cooker.

2. Cover and cook on LOW for 6 to 7 hours* or until the turkey is cooked through.

3. Spoon **about ½ cup** of the turkey mixture down the center of **each** tortilla. Top with the cheese. Fold the tortillas around the filling.

*Or on HIGH for 3 to 4 hours.

Herbed Turkey Breast

Makes 8 servings

Prep Time: **10 minutes**   *Cook Time:* **8 hours**   *Stand Time:* **10 minutes**

---

  1 can (10³/₄ ounces) Campbell's® Condensed Cream of Mushroom Soup
     (Regular *or* 98% Fat Free)

¹/₂ cup water

  4¹/₂- to 5-pound turkey breast

  1 teaspoon poultry seasoning

  1 tablespoon chopped fresh parsley

     Hot mashed potatoes

1. Stir the soup and water in a 3¹/₂- to 6-quart slow cooker. Rinse the turkey with cold water and pat it dry. Rub the turkey with the poultry seasoning and place it into the cooker. Sprinkle with the parsley.

2. Cover and cook on LOW for 8 to 9 hours* or until the turkey is cooked through. Let the turkey stand for 10 minutes before slicing. Serve with the soup mixture and mashed potatoes.

*Or on HIGH for 4 to 5 hours.

Kitchen Tip

If using a frozen turkey breast, thaw it before cooking.

Bacon Potato Chowder

Makes 8 servings

Prep Time: 15 minutes   Cook Time: 3 hours

- 4   slices bacon, cooked and crumbled
- 1   large onion, chopped (about 1 cup)
- 4   cans (10¾ ounces *each*) Campbell's® Condensed Cream of Potato Soup
- 4   soup cans milk
- ¼   teaspoon ground black pepper
- 2   large russet potatoes, cut into ½-inch pieces (about 3 cups)
- ½   cup chopped fresh chives
- 2   cups shredded Cheddar cheese (8 ounces)

1. Stir the bacon, onion, soup, milk, black pepper, potatoes and ¼ *cup* chives in a 6-quart slow cooker.

2. Cover and cook on HIGH for 3 to 4 hours or until the potatoes are tender.

3. Add the cheese and stir until the cheese is melted. Serve with the remaining chives.

Slow-Cooked Taco Shredded Beef

Makes 16 tacos

Prep Time: 10 minutes   *Cook Time: 6 hours*   *Stand Time: 10 minutes*

- 1 can (10^3/$_4$ ounces) Campbell's® Condensed French Onion Soup
- 1 tablespoon chili powder
- ^{1}/$_2$ teaspoon ground cumin
- 2-pound boneless beef chuck roast
- 2 tablespoons finely chopped fresh cilantro leaves
- 16 taco shells
- 1 cup shredded Cheddar cheese (about 4 ounces)
- Shredded lettuce
- Sour cream

1. Stir the soup, chili powder and cumin in a 4-quart slow cooker. Add the beef and turn to coat.

2. Cover and cook on LOW for 6 to 7 hours* or until the beef is fork-tender.

3. Remove the beef from the cooker to a cutting board and let stand for 10 minutes. Using 2 forks, shred the beef. Return the beef to the cooker. Stir the cilantro in the cooker.

4. Spoon **about** ^{1}/$_4$ **cup** beef mixture into **each** taco shell. Top **each** with **about 1 tablespoon** cheese. Top with the lettuce and the sour cream.

Or on HIGH for 4 to 5 hours.

Not Your Gramma's Kugel

Makes 6 servings

Prep Time: 10 minutes   Cook Time: 2 hours

    Vegetable cooking spray

1 package (12 ounces) *uncooked* medium egg noodles (about 7 cups)

$1/2$ cup currants

1 can ($10^3/4$ ounces) Campbell's® Condensed Cheddar Cheese Soup

1 cup cottage cheese

$3/4$ cup sugar

1 teaspoon grated orange zest

2 eggs

1. Spray the inside of a $3^1/2$-quart slow cooker with the cooking spray.

2. Cook the noodles according to the package directions until almost done. Drain and place in the cooker. Sprinkle with the currants.

3. Beat the soup, cottage cheese, sugar, orange zest and eggs in a medium bowl with a fork. Pour over the noodles. Stir to coat.

4. Cover and cook on LOW for 2 to $2^1/2$ hours or until set. Serve warm.

Kitchen Tip

This versatile sweet noodle pudding can be served as a dessert, a brunch dish or a side dish alongside barbecued chicken or brisket.

Coq au Vin

Makes 6 servings

Prep Time: 10 minutes   **Cook Time: 8 hours**

1 package (10 ounces) sliced mushrooms

1 bag (16 ounces) frozen whole small white onions

1 sprig fresh rosemary leaves

2 pounds skinless, boneless chicken thighs **and/or** breasts, cut into 1-inch strips

1/4 cup cornstarch

1 can (10 3/4 ounces) Campbell's® Condensed Golden Mushroom Soup

1 cup Burgundy **or** other dry red wine

Hot mashed **or** oven-roasted potatoes

1. Place the mushrooms, onions, rosemary and chicken into a 3 1/2-quart slow cooker.

2. Stir the cornstarch, soup and wine in a small bowl. Pour over the chicken and vegetables.

3. Cover and cook on LOW for 8 to 9 hours*. Remove the rosemary. Serve with the mashed potatoes.

*Or on HIGH for 4 to 5 hours.

Creamy Blush Sauce with Turkey and Penne

Makes 8 servings

Prep Time: 10 minutes   Cook Time: 7 hours

  4 turkey thighs, skin removed (about 3 pounds)

  1 jar (1 pound 9.75 ounces) Prego® Chunky Garden Mushroom & Green
      Pepper Italian Sauce

 $1/2$ teaspoon crushed red pepper

 $1/2$ cup half-and-half

      Hot cooked tube-shaped pasta (penne)

      Grated Parmesan cheese

1. Put the turkey in a $3^1/2$- to 5-quart slow cooker. Pour the Italian sauce over the turkey and sprinkle with the red pepper.

2. Cover and cook on LOW for 7 to 8 hours* or until the turkey is cooked through. Remove the turkey from the cooker. Remove the turkey meat from the bones and cut it into cubes.

3. Stir the turkey meat and the half-and-half into the cooker. Cover and cook for 10 minutes or until hot. Spoon the turkey mixture over the pasta. Sprinkle with cheese.

Or on HIGH for 4 to 5 hours.

Kitchen Tip

*Substitute **8** bone-in chicken thighs (about 2 pounds) for the turkey thighs. Serves 4.*

Chicken & Bean Burritos

Makes 12 burritos

Prep Time: **10 minutes**   *Cook Time:* **6 hours**

---

1 can (10³/₄ ounces) Campbell's® Condensed Cheddar Cheese Soup

1 teaspoon garlic powder

2 tablespoons chili powder

2 pounds skinless, boneless chicken thighs, cut into 1-inch pieces

1 can (about 14 ounces) black beans, rinsed and drained

1 can (about 14 ounces) pinto beans, rinsed and drained

12 flour tortillas (8- to 10-inch), warmed

Chopped lettuce

Chopped tomato

1. Stir the soup, garlic powder, chili powder and chicken in a 3¹/₂- to 4-quart slow cooker.

2. Cover and cook on LOW for 6 to 7 hours* or until the chicken is cooked through.

3. Mash the black and pinto beans with a fork in a medium bowl. Stir into the chicken mixture. Spoon **about ¹/₂ cup** of the chicken mixture down the center of **each** tortilla. Top with the lettuce and tomato. Fold the tortillas around the filling.

Or on HIGH for 3 to 4 hours.

Melt-in-Your-Mouth Short Ribs

Makes 6 servings

Prep Time: 10 minutes   *Cook Time: 8 hours*

6 serving-sized pieces beef short ribs (about 3 pounds)

2 tablespoons packed brown sugar

3 cloves garlic, minced

1 teaspoon dried thyme leaves, crushed

$1/4$ cup all-purpose flour

1 can (10$1/2$ ounces) Campbell's® Condensed French Onion Soup

1 bottle (12 fluid ounces) dark ale *or* beer

   Hot mashed potatoes *or* egg noodles

1. Place the beef into a 5-quart slow cooker. Add the brown sugar, garlic, thyme and flour and toss to coat.

2. Stir the soup and ale in a small bowl. Pour over the beef.

3. Cover and cook on LOW for 8 to 9 hours* or until the beef is fork-tender. Serve with the mashed potatoes.

Or on HIGH for 4 to 5 hours.

Balsamic Beef with Mushrooms

Makes 6 servings

Prep Time: **15 minutes**   *Cook Time:* **7 hours**

    Vegetable cooking spray

2   pounds boneless beef chuck roast, 1-inch thick

2²/₃ cups Prego® Traditional Italian Sauce

¹/₃ cup balsamic vinegar

2   packages (8 ounces *each*) sliced mushrooms

1   slice bacon, cooked and crumbled

    Hot cooked egg noodles

1. Spray a 10-inch skillet with the cooking spray and heat over medium-high heat for 1 minute. Add the beef and cook until it's well browned on both sides.

2. Stir the Italian sauce, vinegar, mushrooms and bacon in a 5-quart slow cooker. Add the beef and turn to coat.

3. Cover and cook on LOW for 7 to 8 hours* or until the beef is fork-tender. Serve with the egg noodles.

Or on HIGH for 4 to 5 hours.

Slow Cooker Orange Chicken

Makes 4 servings

Prep Time: 10 minutes   Cook Time: 8 hours

1$\frac{1}{2}$ cups Swanson® Chicken Stock

$\frac{1}{4}$ cup teriyaki sauce

3 cloves garlic, minced

$\frac{3}{4}$ cup orange marmalade

4 green onions, sliced (about $\frac{1}{2}$ cup)

2 tablespoons cornstarch

8 chicken thighs, skin removed (about 2 pounds)

$\frac{1}{2}$ cup walnut pieces

Hot cooked rice

1. Stir the stock, teriyaki sauce, garlic, marmalade, **$\frac{1}{4}$ cup** green onions and cornstarch in a 6-quart slow cooker. Add the chicken and turn to coat.

2. Cover and cook on LOW for 8 to 9 hours* or until the chicken is cooked through. Sprinkle with the walnuts and remaining green onions. Serve with the rice.

Or on HIGH for 4 to 5 hours.

Savory Pot Roast

Makes 6 servings

Prep Time: **10 minutes** *Cook Time:* **8 hours**

1 can (10³/₄ ounces) Campbell's® Condensed Cream of Mushroom Soup (Regular *or* 98% Fat Free)

1 pouch (1 ounce) dry onion soup & recipe mix

6 small red potatoes, cut in half

6 medium carrots, cut into 2-inch pieces (about 3 cups)

3- to 3¹/₂-pound boneless beef bottom round roast *or* chuck pot roast

1. Stir the soup, onion soup mix, potatoes and carrots in a 4¹/₂-quart slow cooker. Add the beef and turn to coat.

2. Cover and cook on LOW for 8 to 9 hours* or until the beef is fork-tender.

Or on HIGH for 4 to 5 hours.